C000063158

ENGLISH FOLLIES

JOHN CURTIS

Text by Richard Ashby

SALMON

INTRODUCTION

What is a 'Folly'? Some have defined it as building without any use whatsoever, usually built by a rich man (were any folly builders women?) to adorn his estate. But, in fact, most follies at least have a point, whether it is as somewhere for a pleasant picnic, or to make a statement, to prove a wager, to improve the view or to express a loss. Follies are also about 'feelings'; some are designed to evoke a sense of wonder, or mystery or of horror, others to evoke feelings of beauty or the picturesque.

Although there are some follies dating from the 17th century, there was a plethora of folly building in the 18th. Much of this went hand in hand with the transformation of the formal gardens of the previous centuries into the wonderful artificial landscapes of the great stately homes enlivened with temples, grottoes, columns and bridges. Not all folly buildings are in great gardens though. Some are in industrial cities, or even the suburbs of towns; some dominate their surroundings, others are hidden on lonely hillsides.

Perhaps best of all, follies epitomise the eccentricity in every Englishman and his desire to build and 'improve'. There is little difference in reality between someone who adorns his back garden with a bit of decking, a barbecue, a tiny pond, a sundial, and a spindly pergola, and the great lord who crowns his vista with a Gothic temple and gets there over a Chinese bridge. Perhaps folly building is in our genes!

Gothic Temple, *Stowe, Buckinghamshire*

EYE OF THE NEEDLE,
Wentworth Woodhouse, West Yorkshire
The 2nd Marquess of Rockingham made a drunken bet that he could drive a coach and horse through a needle's eye (in defiance of the saying of Jesus in St Matthew's Gospel). He set about building this elegant triangular structure to prove that he could actually do it.

BRIZLEE TOWER,
Alnwick, Northumberland
When the 1st Duke of Northumberland undertook the restoration of Alnwick Castle in the late 18th century, the grounds were landscaped by 'Capability' Brown and included a number of follies. This one, built in 1777, was designed by Robert Adam. It is said to have been inspired by the creation of the Duke's pastry cook.

WITCH HOUSE, *Hestercombe*, *Somerset*
In an age of religious piety and admiration for the rational virtues of Greece, the inclusion of a Witch House would have been designed to evoke feelings of gloom and perhaps dread. This thatched house is built of wood and the branches are twisted into fantastic shapes. Inside are figures of the witch on her broomstick, her cat and an owl.

CHINESE DAIRY, *Woburn*, *Bedfordshire*
The passion for Arcadian landscapes also led to the idealisation of the rural way of life. If only bored ladies could live as simply as milkmaids! The fashion probably started with Marie Antoinette at Versailles, but England was affected too. In Woburn's 1790s Dairy this romantic ideal is expressed in the newly fashionable Chinese style.

SHAM CASTLE,
Wimpole, Cambridgeshire
Sanderson Miller, a great designer of sham
castles, built one for the Lord Chancellor
of England, on the hill opposite his house.
It has a massive four-storied tower, skilfully
broken to give an air of great age.

LEPTIS MAGNA COLUMNS,
Virginia Water, Surrey
The remains of the Roman Temples at Leptis
Magna, in what is now Tripoli, were displayed
in the courtyard of the British Museum in
1821. George IV had them moved here and
arranged in a picturesque fashion.

TURKISH TENT,
Painshill, Surrey

Travellers brought back with them ideas which were incorporated into the fashionable gardens of the day. This 18th century Turkish Tent, draped in blue and white canvas was reconstructed in 1993 from contemporary pictures of the garden.

CODGER'S FORT,
Cambo, Northumberland

Thomas Wright of County Durham was an astronomer who was also interested in garden design and architecture. He was responsible for building a number of follies for his wealthy patrons including this sham castle which echoes the real forts of the border country.

JACK THE TREACLE EATER,
Barwick, Somerset

The most fanciful of the four boundary markers of Barwick Park is this rubble-built cone surmounted by a statue of Mercury, the messenger of the gods. There is a legend that the statue commemorates the achievements of a family messenger whose training diet included large amounts of treacle!

THE SUGAR LOAF,
Brightling, East Sussex

Perhaps as a result of over-indulgence at dinner, 'Mad' Jack Fuller wagered that he could see the spire of Dallington Church from his dining room. Morning showed that a hill was in the way so he immediately set to and had a cone-shaped replica spire built which could be clearly seen. He won his bet!

THE VICARAGE,
Morwenstow, Cornwall

The Reverend Robert Hawker was, for 41 years in the middle of the 19th century, Vicar of Morwenstow on the remote north coast of Cornwall. He was known for his poetry (he wrote the *'Song of the Western Men'*) and is credited with the introduction of the harvest festival service into the Church of England. He was an eccentric, smoking opium in a little hut he built on the cliff edge. He sat watching the sea and looking out for ships in danger on the rocky coast, raising the alarm and helping in the rescue. Five of the chimneys on his vicarage are in the style of church towers he particularly admired, the sixth, the kitchen chimney, is a copy of his mother's tomb. Perhaps this is not really a folly, but it is a very suitable house for just such a man.

TRIANGULAR LODGE,
Rushton, Northamptonshire

Sir Thomas Tresham's 1594 Triangular Lodge is a statement of his faith, he was a convert to Roman Catholicism. Everything is in threes, the mystical number signifying the Holy Trinity. The three sides each measures 33 ft, there are three stories, the roof has three gables with three pinnacles on each side and each wall is decorated with stone carvings of geometric patterns, all in threes.

THE CHURCH OF ST LAWRENCE,
West Wycombe, Buckinghamshire
In 1762, Sir Francis Dashwood, Chancellor of the Exchequer, had this golden sphere placed atop the tower of the church. It is big enough to hold at least six people and Sir Francis and his 'Hell Fire Club' supposedly used it for drinking and gambling.

HOUSE IN THE CLOUDS,
Thorpeness, Suffolk
Some follies have no discernible practical use, while others are practical buildings disguised as something else. Thorpeness was built in the 1920s as a holiday village in the Tudor style for those seeking relaxation and was free of cinemas, piers and everything else which made many seaside resorts noisy and crowded. As the surrounding area is flat, the problem arose as to how to store the water the visitors needed without building something unsightly. The solution was this 'House in the Clouds', a weather-boarded, 1920s house with a steep pitched roof, chimney and windows concealing a 30,000 gallon water tank, raised on a five-story tower which contains a real house. Thorpeness is now on mains water. Where the water tank once was is now additional living space.

DRUIDS' TEMPLE,
Swinton, *North Yorkshire*

Many people in the 18th century
were fascinated by the Druids and
their supposed pre-Christian religion
in Britain. It was no doubt for this
reason that the owner of Swinton Hall,
William Danby, whilst also seeking to
relieve the desperate unemployment
of the area, had this massive
'Stonehenge' built on the Yorkshire
moors. It is complete with massive
standing stones, altars, a ceremonial
avenue and a small cave. Legend has
it that Danby offered to provide an
income and food for anyone who could
live as a hermit in his temple for seven
years, not cutting his hair or speaking
to anyone. Some tried but the longest
anyone could manage was four and a half
years before being defeated by the
elements and the isolation.

TATTINGSTONE WONDER,
Tattingstone, *Suffolk*

Edward White, the local squire of this quiet
East Anglian village, decided that he would give
his villagers something to wonder at. From the
road it appears to be a pretty flint-built church.
But from behind it is revealed as a row of
cottages with an incongruous three-sided tower
with no roof and open on the fourth side.
It is one of the most famous follies in England.

SHARK IN THE ROOF,
Headington, Oxfordshire

This amazing shark, installed in 1986, very much upset the City Council who refused permission. In a rare display of common sense and sympathy for its quirkiness, a Government inspector allowed the appeal. One has to wonder how many other follies in this book would have got planning permission if they were erected today.

BURTON PYNSENT STEEPLE,
Curry Rivel, Somerset

William Pitt the elder, himself a leading 18th century politician and father of the youngest and longest serving prime minister that England has ever had, was left the estate of Burton Pysent in the will of an admirer, Sir William Pynsent. After fighting off the claims of the disinherited family, Pitt set about making major improvements to the estate and had this Tuscan column erected by 'Capability' Brown in thanks to his benefactor whom he had never met. In the 1940s a cow twice managed to climb the internal stairs and was persuaded to return to safety. She finally made it to the top on a third attempt and plunged to her death.

HORSE MONUMENT,
Farley Mount, Hampshire
'Beware Chalk Pit' was the curious name given to a horse which leapt into a 25ft deep chalk pit on the Hampshire Downs without harming its owner, who was out fox-hunting. The horse was entered for the Hunter's Plate trophy under the name at races on Worthy Down and went on to win.

ASHTON MEMORIAL,
Williamson Park, Lancaster, Lancashire
Erected in 1907, this enormous, but useless, structure is a classic folly. With a huge dome, Portland stone cupolas, columns and pediments, all in a heavy neo-baroque style, it is an architectural *tour de force*. It commemorates one of the wives of Lord Ashton, a rich manufacturer of linoleum.

PAGODA, *Kew, London*

This pagoda is one of the earliest Chinese buildings in England and it inspired many others. It was built in 1761 for Princess Augusta who founded the famous botanical garden on her estate. It was formerly even more ornate than as seen today with dragons, covered with multi-covered glass, on the roofs and 80 bells which were sounded by the wind.

SHAM CASTLE, *Bath, Somerset*

Ralph Allen, the developer of Georgian Bath, had this so-called 'eye-catcher' built to punctuate the view from his town house in Old Lilliput Alley. The house is now obscured by later buildings, but the Sham Castle survives. It is frequently floodlit and continues to catch the eye from the city below.

GATE HOUSE,
Castle Howard, North Yorkshire

Castle Howard is a magnificent 'palace' set in an equally splendid landscaped park, which is dotted with fine buildings and protected by a fortified wall. This fantastic gatehouse was designed by Sir John Vanbrugh (who also designed the great house) and was used as a guest house for visiting gentry.

TENANTRY COLUMN,
Alnwick, Northumberland

The end of the Napoleonic wars brought about a catastrophic fall in agricultural prices. The Duke of Northumberland reduced his rents and his grateful tenants raised this column in thanks. However, the Duke thought that if they could afford such a generous gesture they could afford his rents, and raised them again. The column is also known as the 'Farmer's Folly'!

WAINHOUSE TOWER,
Halifax, West Yorkshire

This is an industrial folly. John Wainhouse planned this chimney to take the smoke away from his Halifax dye works. He sold the works in 1874 but the new owner refused to buy the incomplete chimney so Wainhouse had it finished as an observatory. It was also said that he used it to keep an eye on his hated neighbour.

EYE-CATCHER,
Mow Cop, Cheshire

An 'eye-catcher' is designed to draw the eye and perhaps to improve the view, often from a nearby house. The sham castle at Mow Cop or Mole Cop was placed on its hill to be viewed from nearby Rode Hall. 'Primitive' Methodism began here with a great open air meeting in 1807.

GROTTO, *Hawkstone*, *Shropshire*

The poet, Alexander Pope, was an early writer on the idea of the landscape garden and his garden at Twickenham was hugely influential. It was divided by a road and Pope joined the two parts with a tunnel, which he ornamented as a romantic and exotic addition to his garden. It was much imitated and grottoes became an essential feature of many gardens. The grotto at Hawkstone Park is a veritable labyrinth which may have originated as a copper mine but which was extended and decorated in the mid-18th century. It is notable for the stone columns left to support the roof. There are windows cut into the side and a terrace from which to enjoy the view.

GROTTO, *Clifton*, *Bristol*

Thomas Goldney was a prosperous Bristol merchant whose garden at Goldney House contains a beautiful pillared grotto begun in 1737 but not completed for over 20 years. Its walls are lined with coral and thousands of shells and the pillars are covered with amethysts, jasper, agate and the quartz crystals known as Bristol 'diamonds'.

PALLADIAN BRIDGE, *Wilton, Wiltshire*

Water is an essential feature of any classical or landscaped garden and where there is water there should be a bridge. The bridge doesn't necessarily have to lead anywhere but it must be picturesque. The Palladian Bridge at Wilton House, near Salisbury was built in 1737 and is based on an unexecuted plan for the Rialto in Venice. It was much admired and copied several times elsewhere

Published in Great Britain by J. Salmon Ltd., Sevenoaks, Kent TN13 1BB. Telephone 01732 452381. Email enquiries@jsalmon.co.uk.
Design by John Curtis. Text and photographs © John Curtis. All rights reserved. No part of this book may be produced, stored in a retrieval system or transmitted in any form or by any means without prior written permission of the publishers.
ISBN 1-84640-037-6 Printed in Slovenia © 2006

Title page photograph: Shobdon Arches, *Herefordshire*
Front cover photograph: Broadway Tower, *Worcestershire*. Back cover photograph: Chesterton Windmill, *Warwickshire*